LEVITATE

THROUGH LIFE

POOJA SHEKHAR

ISBN 979-888530659-1

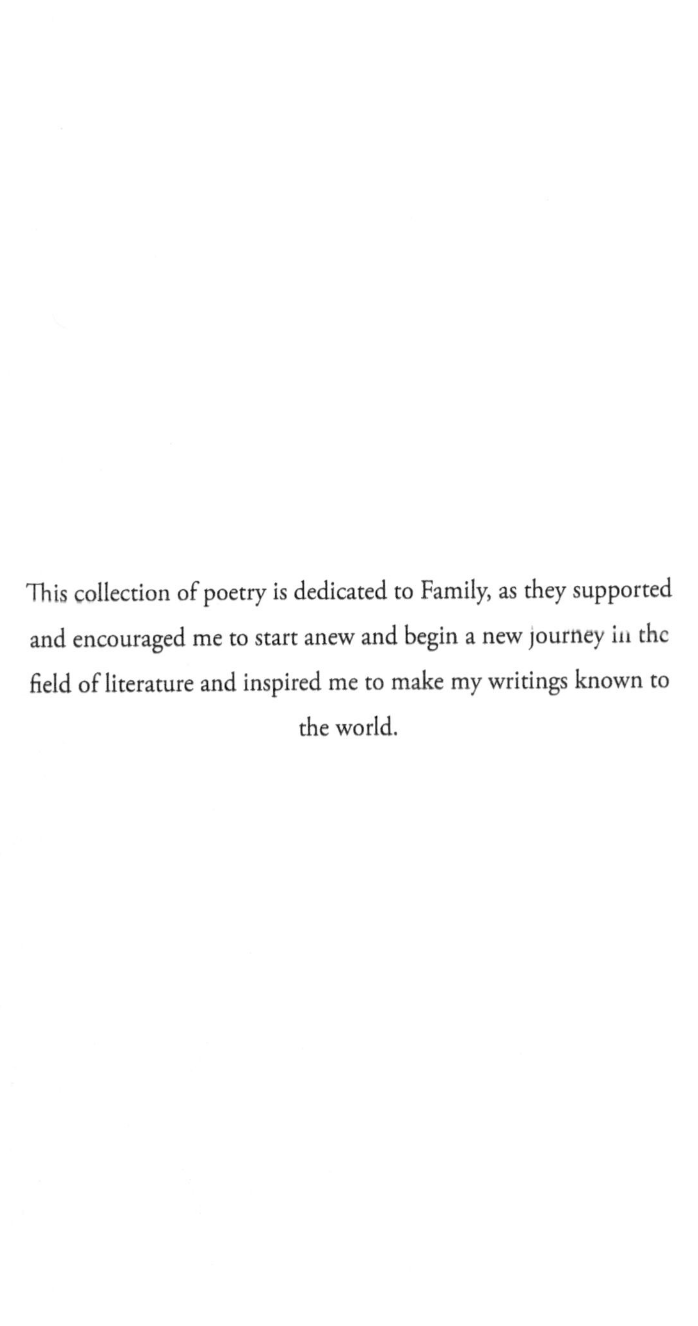

This collection of poetry is dedicated to Family, as they supported and encouraged me to start anew and begin a new journey in the field of literature and inspired me to make my writings known to the world.

Contents

Foreword

The book contains the inner world of the writer. Something all of us posses but is barely known to the world outside of us. The Author showcases their inner most desires and feelings and mostly thoughts flowing by.

Preface

This collection of poems mostly have melancholy in them. It's the words that can't be spoken but can be written. The poems are an after effect of certain situations in life and are derived from them. They are mostly feelings put into words. Trying to express the inner most desires and feelings using words are not easy but is still worth a try.

Acknowledgements

I would like to thank everyone involve in the making of this book. Firstly my Mother she has been a constant support encouraging me to write and publish and my sister for being an inspiration and an example for me to write this book.

I am also thankful to my poet friends as they inspired me and because of their inspiration i was able to write. And my publisher for giving me a platform to share my works with the world.

1. A Winter's Morning

The cool breeze
The dark night
That comfort of solitude
That beauty of a book
Leaning back on the windowpane
Wrapped up in the cosy wool
The moon looks at her
And asked
Do I look so beautiful?
Slowly the comfort
Of the dark night faded
Bringing forth a bright light
Piercing through the laziness
A reminder of a new start
As the sky burned
The snow glimmered
The trees danced
The birds took flight
Winter became more
More than everyone hoped for
More than the cold season
More than the leafless trees

LEVITATE

It resembled a hope
A hope of families
A hope of friends
The hope of love & laughter
And of showering lights
The shimmering light of the snow
An announcement
For everyone to gather
To look at each other
Smile & be grateful
For their families, friends
For their lives & laughter
The fragrance spread wide
Reaching out to people
Beyond the suns light
A reminder to forgive
A reminder to remember
To see each other in a new light
The rays fell down
On smiles and laughter
Melting the cold snow
Warming the morning tea
Raising the temperature
A little at a time
As the winter morning shined bright
More people started to pass by
They looked around the houses covered in snow

They looked around the beaming light
Sunrise they said
"The most beautiful time of the day"
The presence of the sun
Felt more alive
As that special someone passed by
The sun made him look brighter
The winter made him look colder
She thought to herself
"Only if the sunrise during a winter
Could be person
Then he would be it"
Looking at the bright beautiful light
The boy thought to himself
"Only if this moment could stay forever"
The snow started to melt
The cool breeze said "hello"
With the sky livelier than before
The season felt special
The scent of old furniture
Pleasing to everyone
Brought everyone together
The morning at its end
The day yet to began
Slowly people laughing
Started getting serious
Looked at the clock

Closed the doors
The locked doors could not protect
The winter thief
Coldness passed through the walls
The light pierced through the windows
Occupying empty houses with their presence
The houses stood lonely
With each other in silence
Yearning for their residents
In the cold season
The children locked up in classrooms
The adults locked up in offices
Looked out the windows
Only to admire
The brightness
The warmth the winter brings with it
Thinking "only if winter was a place
One could visit and leave at will"
The season brought gifts
That shined brightly in the light
A symbol of hope
Of love and belonging
Like a winter's morning

2. Cage Of Love

Our opinions and thinking
Completely different
You believe in something different
And I believe in something different
Falling down is not my fear
My dream doesn't take birth from some fear
It takes birth from pure love
Which in your eyes
Is pure suffering
If it's a wing for you
Then I would rather cut my own wings
Never take a flight
And choose to suffer
Only if it means
That I can make my dreams come true
Even if being alone means suffering for you
I would rather suffer
Than live in the cage of love

3. Done

Done for this life
Done for this pain
Done for all the feelings
Done for all the mess
Now there's no sorrow
There's no happiness
Now the world doesn't exist
And yet still it does
Now there's no looking back
No seeing
No more keeping your eyes closed
And ignoring the truth
What lies ahead is a myth
But with more curiosity
No more blindness all is all and nothing at all
The truth, the reality
Which only few can see.

4. Empath's Rage

What do I have to do?
In order to not be bothered by others
To make myself completely numb
To the world outside of me
To be nothing
But a tool
For the duties
I have to complete
To find a place
Where no one
Chains me down
A place where
No one cages me in
A place
Where freedom is neither given nor taken
It's abundant
What do I have to do to belong?
To be free
This world is full of people
Trying to prove themselves,
People
Who are determined

LEVITATE

What they're doing is the right thing
Without even considering
The collateral damage
Caused by the fight they're trying to win
Such lack of empathy
Causes the rage the anger
To the empaths
That when starts burning
Consumes everything
And in the end
We are left
With this selfish materialistic world
To live in

5. Good Night

Good night
To my soul
To my love
This world exists
For everyone
But me
The peace
The quiet
The silence
Steals my heart
While piercing it with a knife
Everything is gone
Everyone is gone
Good night
To my soul
To my love

6. HeartBreak

Found my heart
My soul
In you
Lost my soul
My heart
To you
Hard to see
Impossible to define
The truth unrevealed
Tears streaming down
The cheeks burning hot red
The fire lighting up her eyes
Showing the anger that's hidden inside
The sadness shower
The disappointment craves
The anger burns
With lightning glaze
Shined brighter than the sun
Now lost all of its shine
She kept her heart
Shielded in armor,
Because she thought

That was the only way
To keep it
From breaking, ever again.

7. Runaway

I just want to runaway
To a faraway place
Where no one can find me
Where there is only peace and quiet
A place with no judgment to pass
A place with no race to win
A calming and quiet place
A serene and peaceful atmosphere
Not to hide
Not to devise
But only to live by
If possible in love & peace
The world has no such place
The world has no such race
It only encourages ravaging
It only encourages savages
The truth of the world hides
While the lies live subsides
Becoming just another thing
People happily live by
So soon they thought
So soon they wondered

Why can't it entertain us more?
Why can't it tolerate pain more?
Only to amuse
I live by
Only entertain
I survive

8. Life Passing By

The world has never been quieter
The world has never been brighter
This world was never mine
This world will never be mine
Lost in the sound
Kept me bound
To this earth
To this mirth
Words found me
Silence bound me
To see is to be blind
To love is to unwind
The most conflicting thoughts
The most reflective thoughts
This was the beauty of mind
This was the beauty of the soul
Sounds became distant
Wounds became infected
People saw
People left
Nobody cares about the ones in pain
In pain, they wept and cried all in vain

Saw people pass by
Saw people living their lives
Only if they thought
Only if they lived
Hope was lost
Hope was found
They looked at the sky
And wondered why
Why do we live the pain
While others live in vain?

9. Meaningless

Everything in this world
Has the same meaning
It's people living in daydreams
Trying to prove otherwise
All words
Have the same meaning
It's us humans
Pretending
They have different meanings
Words possess no true meaning
They're simply sounds
That animal called humans to make to communicate...
Being speechless or having many words
In the end, has no meaning at all
All languages
Have the same meaning
It's us humans
Pretending
They have different meanings
What one calls rubbish?
What one calls worthy
In the end

Are all the same
Having the same origin
The same meaning
It's us humans
Who pretends
That different sound
Have different meanings

10. Night-Time

Days are dreamy
Filled with the societal illusions
Nights are real
Where people uncover themselves and are free
It's the shower of the moon the stars
The cool breeze blowing by
Making me feel tipsy
On words and letters
Giving my feelings a window to sit by
I hope sleep finds me enchanting
So that I would be able hide
Nights are never allowed to others
To enter my domain
For the writer in me possesses me at night
And haunts the world sleeping by
The songs of the night are better left unsung
So let me fall asleep
Let the music inside me die
Not in vein but in pain
Of being unable to live during the day
To see the light
And shine bright

I would be conscious and unable to write
Sleep wanders off with every moment of life
Cause death wanders its way through to me

11. Reincarnation Of Hell

Though the world is lost
Though there's nothing to live for
I refuse to die in vain
I refuse to leave the earth
Until I see the pain
The hurt
The suffering
Reflected by this world
For the world
To see the unknown
This world should become
What it has never know
The unknown
Which it fears
Until it becomes known
The unknown which
It kills
The fear of being unknown
The unknown, it wants to know
The unknown it craves to be
For the god's in heaven
Have blessed my wish

To see this world in tears
To see this moment perish
To see what it's like to suffer
For your world gave me this place only
Flooded with tears
Perishable moments
Hell like suffering
For this world is a reincarnation of hell itself
Maybe not for you
But at the very least for me

12. Smile

I can see myself
It's not bad...
It's just peaceful and calm....
And incredibly beautiful...
I know where I am going after all...
I have got it all figured out...
Even if there is delay
I am going to get there...
People believe
That they need support
And that they're weak
Cause nobody
Is there for them...
Instead of realizing
That in reality
Nobody has ever been supporting you...
You're on your own...
We've got this situation we're in
Only because nobody else would've handled it better
And we could not be our best version
Even if it was a little better
Or even if it was a little worse

The wounds won't rot...
I have seen it cure by my methods...
It's just that every day
Brings something new...
And the more adversities I experience
The better I become...
What shouldn't be done...
What should be done...
How to avoid this...
How to attract that ...
It brings out the positive in me...
Somehow!
If I had a better life
I guess
I would've been
A selfish, arrogant, ignorant, moody girl...
I am just honest
Even if somebody else is going through the same thing
They would say everything is fine and lie...
While I have guts to say
'No my life's a mess and still I am able to do great'
And smile and be happy

13. Society

Thrust upon thee silence
While everyone speaks
Thrust upon thee love
While everyone hates
Thrust upon thee kindness
While everyone mistakes
Judges my life
For whom I am
Calls upon me
For whom they see me to be
Speaks about me for
Who they know me to be with others

14. Stripped

They stripped me down
Of love
Of hope
Of hate
Of respect
They stripped me down
Of courage
Of rage
Of character
Of happy ever after
They stripped me down
Of words
Of world
Of pain
Of sane
They stripped me down
To the core
Naked
Bare skin
Flesh clearer than the bright sky
They stripped me down
Of rights

Of duties
Of friendships
Of relationships
They stripped me down
Of peace
Of health
Of intelligence
Of excellence
They couldn't strip down
The conviction in me
The strength in me
The vulnerable me
The indestructible me

15. Tragedy

Through pain and sorrow
i vowed to accompany you with my life
But here I am
Taking your life
In order to save mine
What a tragedy this life is
To live in a world like this
Hell will be my home
Satan would be my companion
The hell's fire will light my kitchen
I'll haunt you to the very end of this world
Tormenting you
Reminding you
Of what you owe me
While enjoying the hell's wine made of blood

16. Chaos

I did not wanted to hear the chaos,
But the world didn't change
Instead I must go deaf
To stop the chaos
Cause I am weak
Powerless to Stop the Chaos
I go deaf
Impossible to make the world understand me
I understood the world
By going deaf
The world so cruel so rigid worships nothing but Ego
I lost
I submitted by going deaf
The beautiful sounds I wished to hear
Never existed
The only sounds heard were the unstoppable chaos
Powerless
Not wanting to listen
I go deaf
The weak
Never given a thought
Pays the price for the powerful

This world has nothing to give
Only to take
Slowly it's taking my dream
Of listening to the beautiful sounds
Which I never found
Away from me
The obstinate world,
Never listening,
So cruel,
So rigid,
Worships ego,
Unable to Stop the Chaos,
Defeated,
I stopped hearing
Powerless,
Paying the price for the powerful,
I stopped hearing,
This world only takes & takes,
Taking away the only dream,
The Angelic Sounds,
Suppressed,
Amongst the Chaos,
I stopped hearing.
People use their voices
To make noise
While they should be creating sounds.

17. Darker Than Black

My favourite colour is black...
Only if I could find a colour
Darker than Black
Because I feel at ease
In the darkness
Where no one can see me
No one can judge me
No one can hurt me
Cause it's too dark
The colour of black
In which no one can find me

18. Purpose

Lost in the thoughts
Of finding the purpose of this world around me
Wondering
To whom it serves?
To whom it prays?
To whom it asks for forgiveness?
To whom it wishes to?
The purpose...
What is its purpose?
Is it just to inhabit humans?
Animals?
The man-made world?
The nature that's left?
What is its purpose?
Is it to protect the sun?
Or to be burned by it someday?
Or just to disappear?
As there won't be any creatures left
To know that this planet it's earth.

19. Two Worlds

Two worlds
Parted from each other
Looking into each other's eyes
They found peace and solace
Saw the world behind them
This made them look weaker
But still, they parted
Because if they stood together
They might collide
The stars,
The sky
Cried in vain
Nothing was to be lost
Nothing was to be found
All they had was themselves
But were living
In an illusion
Of having each other